Napkin Poetry

A Collection of Poetry
by
Jennifer-Crystal Johnson

First printing: July 2010.
ISBN 978-0-982-85870-7

Printed and bound in the United States.

Book Cover Design by Jennifer-Crystal Johnson
www.JenniferCrystalJohnson.com

Broken Publications
A Pacific Northwest
Publisher

www.BrokenPublications.com

I fondly dedicate this book to all the midnight coffee-campers in coffee shops and diners around the world.

When 4:00 AM rolls around and you're wired on about three pots of gut-rot coffee, scribbling on napkins or in notebooks, or goofing around with friends...

Remember that these times, no matter how insignificant they may seem at the moment, are priceless...

Cherish every caffeine-inspired bit of it.

=)

Connect with Jen Online

Facebook:
https://www.facebook.com/JenniferCrystalJohnson/

Twitter:
https://twitter.com/brokenpoet

YouTube:
https://www.youtube.com/user/TheBrokenPoetJen

Amazon:
http://amzn.to/2cLsTOp

Other Books by Jennifer-Crystal Johnson

Fibers, book 1 of the Infiltration Trilogy
Science Fiction, Broken Publications 2016

Our Capacity for Evil, short stories
Horror, Broken Publications 2015

The Ten Pillars of a Happy Relationship
Personal Development, Broken Publications, 2014

If You're Human Don't Open the Door, short stories
Creature Horror, Broken Publications 2012

Strangers with Familiar Faces
Poetry, Broken Publications 2012

Also check out:

Soul Vomit: Beating Domestic Violence
Anthology, Broken Publications 2012

Soul Vomit: Domestic Violence Aftermath
Anthology, Broken Publications 2014

Table of Contents

Will You Be

Eating at my flesh
Dissolving all I am
Infecting every gash
Blood flowing from my hands

I've tried to break free
From this prison I call me
I've tried breaking down the door
But I just hurt myself more

Gnawing at my brain
I cannot heal the pain
I cannot dull the hurt
I can't ignore your words

The more I try to fight it
The stronger it becomes
But if I just ignore it
I hate the feeling numb

So what can I do
To kill the pain inside?
I want to hear the truth
Find purity past the lies

Will you be pure and true for me?
Will you be my honesty?
Will you be
The innocence I need?

Make Me

Make me your purity
Make me your meaning
Make me your everything
Make me your life

You'll be my somebody
You'll be my sanity
You'll be my craziness
You'll be my love

Make me your royalty
Make me your normalcy
Make me your lover
And I'll make you mine

You'll be my everything
I'll be your all

A Drive in the Dark

My hands are loosely resting
On a large brown steering wheel.
There is loud,
Sensually rhythmic music
Pounding from my speakers.

I am alone.

It is dark, the only light
Shining onto the road
From my headlights.

The narrow back road
Stretches out in front of me,
No signs of life to be seen.

The trees look like they have silver tips,
Illuminated edges,
And in the mirror
It is black.

An erotically smooth male voice
Makes my ears overflow with pleasure.

The rhythmic pounding
Of a deep bass drum
Becomes more and more

Insistent,

More and more

Intense,

Until, finally,
With one last effort to be overpowering,
The song's climax is reached
With a deafening orgasm of sound,
And all goes dark and silent.

I awoke in a ditch.

Innocently Watching

I have now become lost
In the floor,
The walls,
The ceiling,
And the artwork therein….

I'm drifting along in this dream,
When suddenly
The appearance of too many
Strangers with familiar faces
Wakes me up from my trance….

Within a few seconds,
The strangers, the blemishes on my art,
Have left again,
And I re-enter
The floor, the ceiling, the walls….

Until all I do is watch,
Listen, and observe,
Trying to blend into everyone
While still keeping my own identity….

It's no use. I am lost again.
I go unnoticed,
And, therefore,
I escape from real life unharmed,
Complete, and unscathed….

I am still
Innocently watching.

Never Look Back

Nothing matters anymore
All I want to do is run away
Across the world to find my core
Fulfill my dreams and be okay

I want to know that I am free
To feel it burning through my veins
Be everything I want to be
With only myself to obey

Are you here? Are you with me?
Can't be sure, for I don't know me
Take some time to search again
I find myself in everything

This races through my mind
At least once or twice a day
Nothing's real and nothing's mine
And I never really have a say

So what's a better way for me
To find myself within this place
To truly feel alive and free
To bring to surface my real face

Than leave from here without regret
To find a me I can't forget
To run away…
… Never looking back.

Perception

Chilled to the bone
By my own thoughts
I'm never, ever home
Alone, yet I am not

My finger is bleeding
My mouth is sore
I don't feel like leaving
But I can't ignore

The sound of the voice
In the back of my mind
I haven't a choice
Besides being kind

I feel all the tension
Surrounding the world
I can never mention
What begs to be told

How do you feel?
You say, but you don't
You cannot be real
So maybe you aren't

Helpless and sad
So angry am I
Because you feel bad.

Crumbling

Beat her down...
Lean on her until
She finally gives,
Collapsing to nothing
But bits and pieces
Of a complex puzzle
With no one there
To put her back together,
To build her up again
So they can beat her down
Once more

Dead and then
Brought back to life
By everyone
Who's ever needed her
For anything at all,
Only to find that
Her mind is no longer
Complete or awake

The purity gone
The innocence lost
Her honesty stolen from her
And trampled upon
By so many friends
So many lovers
So many strangers

Simply to redeem
Their non-existent
Dignity

No One Knows

Keep your eyes on the road
Unless it's deserted
Smile and pretend
That everything's fine

Even when it isn't
Even when nothing matters
Even when you're ending
Even when you're all alone
In a sea of nameless people
Strangers with familiar faces

Because everyone looks the same
No one is unique
And no one is special
Because everyone copies someone
And nothing is real
And no one is genuine
Unless they try to be

This is the rarest treasure
Because everyone has a façade
We all wear a mask
But how many layers are there
When you don't even know
Who you are

You try to protect yourself
By playing pretend
For everyone else
But everyone needs someone
And no one truly knows anyone

Needing Contentment

Dig my hollow, empty grave
I will swallow all you gave
As to darkness I'm enslaved
Knowing nothing can be saved

I wish that I could radiate
All my anger, pain, and hate
Accepting every horrid fate
And wishing you would try a taste

My patience now is wearing thin
And nothing could be everything
Feel my vengeance, deep it stings
To the shred of light I'll cling

Nothing hopes and nothing prays
Wanting everything but praise
Surrounded by a grayish haze
I'm lost in someone's endless maze

I will not find my way nor try
Because the tears still fall from eyes
But nothing matters, no one cries
Except for me and all that dies

The silent screams from deep inside
My core is nothing when it hides
I do not know, I can't decide
Can I not be content, although I've tried?

Die For Purity

I'd like to paint
With my fingertips
Abstract emotions
While feeling the tools
Squirm through my fingers

And knowing that I
Am the only truth
The only reality
Among chaos
To be the order
The sanity
In the psych ward
An odd collection
Of perfection

Something among nothing
Someone among
All the nobodies
So how do I surface
When all this shit
Covers and hides me
Like a sheet of ice

I can make you see

So would it be worth it
To fall through the ice
And drown, and die
If the only thing you gain
Is the purity
Of truth?

Connecting Me

Rainbow sunrise
In the middle of the night
Brightest colors
Surrounded by the dark
Nothing to
Describe the feelings
Racing through my veins
Infecting every pore
Connecting all of me

I am one with myself

And I wish
There was no one
To rip me from me

And I wish
There was someone
To hold me together

When I start
To fall apart

My Equal

I sit and I watch
And I wait and I bleed
Ready for anything,
Wanting it all
And fearing nothing
Until I take the fall

The world is mine
Because I make it so
And the people therein
Are my slaves, and I know

That they are below
And I am above
Until I find my equal
I cannot feel love

And everything matters
But nothing is true
And everyone lies
But takes offense when I do

Beautiful Moment

Needles penetrating
Every part of my body
Until satisfaction
Decides that it's time

For the release
Of a thousand screams
A million sighs
And a billion sensations

As the birth and death
And decay of a moment
Rips everything apart
And puts it back together

Within a single second,
There is nothing left until later
But the bliss of the birth
And death
And decay of that moment

All That Matters

Break down the barriers
Of conversation
Of the beautiful
And unreal thought

That no one
Is ever worth trusting

So why spiral downward
If the hole is that vast

How can you know
What lies in the deep
If all you do
Is only shallow

And all you say
Untrue

There are no emotions
That stem from the surface
They come from below

And if you feel many
You let yourself drown
In all that will ever
Really matter

Curious Fingers

The end is always
The beginning
And the bad
Exceeds the good
But makes it more
Delicious

Death is the birth
Of something new and fresh
So all the words
Will flow together into thoughts
Once I kill
The source of nothingness
And boredom is no more

Something has peeled back
And the skin
Of what is never real
Has been stripped away
And picked at
By my own curious fingers

And the flesh beneath
Is all I want to be

Mosaic

I'd like to be
Intrigued by someone.

Be a little wild,
Feel a little free,
Be a little crazy,
Find a deeper me.

In the climax
Of the addiction,
This is who I am…

A simple person,
Hard to understand,
Easy to see through
Unless the things I do
Confuse you.

A light in the dark,
But a mere shadow in light
Because I don't shine
Quite brightly enough
To be seen in the sun.

A walking muse for some,
A comforting shoulder for others,
And a mosaic of thoughts
For myself.

Colorful
Black and white.

Indecisive Lover

Inspiration
Or lack thereof
Can rip me to pieces,
Eating me up
And chewing my mind to a pulp,
Then spitting me out again,
Using me only
For a short while

Then tossing me aside
Like an inconsistent
And indecisive lover….

If I force it,
All that comes out
Is shit,
But if I don't
At least tempt it,
There isn't anything at all.

I am attached
And in love with Inspiration,
And I am at its
Beckon call.

If it doesn't
Want me anymore,
I have infinite patience
Until it does.

Distorted

Swirls of color and blackness
Dance around in front of my face
Translucent
So I can still see you

But your faces are wavy
And much too distorted
So I can't tell
What's really beautiful

Sounds of all shapes
Layers of music and noise
Filter into my ears
And eventually to my thoughts

But, unless I focus, I cannot
Decide what is real

For the layers of lies
Contort the voices
Making them painfully
Out of tune

Vanish

Left bare
When all illusions
Are stripped away
And the physical aspect
Matters no more
Than yesterday's gossip

Naked and cold
And bruised to the bones
The muscles detach
And the heart as well

The mind left alone
Unfeeling, thus empty
For all that has mattered
Is gone away now

So, left unattended
This creature, this being
Could vanish
To nothing

Numbness

No real comfort… nothing true.
Others' lies discourage me.
I try to be an optimist,
But I don't like what I see.

I'm drowning in an ocean
Of feelings I don't know,
And no one's here to save me;
I don't know where to go.

My logic and stability
Have left me far behind;
I don't know what you think of me,
But I don't really mind.

A comfort in the numbness,
I don't know what I want.
Should I really try to feel
When all I'll do is hurt?

I just feel like falling,
Giving up on everything.
It's tempting me, it's calling,
I don't know what it'll bring….

Sharing Me

Waiting in anticipation
For the moment I can feel
Connecting with the instrument
And one with my voice

All the sounds are mingling
Mixing together to form
Pure perfection
Bliss in harmony
With beauty and grace

My mind is finally at peace
When my fingers move
Weightlessly across the keys
No distractions
Nothing can break the spell
Except the song's end

But even then I am content
As the applause is for me
Whether it be exterior
Or only in my head
It is always for me

For I have accomplished
Radiating myself
Parts of my soul floating about
With the notes and the voice

And filling everything

The Only Thing

...And I became convinced
That there is
Nothing left to know
But time,
And time won't change

For it is steady
And it's always
The only thing
To know

And the only thing
That's true

For how many times
Has a clock
Lied to you?

Amplified

Nothing without
No one within
Stealing my breath
Taking my sin
Or making it stronger

Amplify me
Screaming
Amplify me
Dying
Radiate my
Insides
Put them on a
Slide projector
Or smear them on a
Big white movie screen
For all the world to see

And yet I feel no shame
No embarrassment
No anger, guilt, or fear
Do you
Feel for me?
Or at least the blood
Decorating white...
Do you feel for it?

It's me,
Do you recall?

In Pieces

I woke up in pieces
All over you

And the part of me
That could still think
Wondered
What you did to me

Slowly, you woke up
And decided to
Put me back together
But you did it wrong!

You messed it up!

How will you explain this
To my savior
When he gets here?

I still don't know
What is what
Or who
Or where I am

But maybe
I can do it myself
Without help
And wake up whole
Tomorrow

The Bluest Sky

Could you please just
Go away?
I want to hide
And never stay

And though it all
Makes nothing real
I want to fall
And never heal

I don't know why
I'm not sure how
The bluest sky
Can still fall down

And simple beauty
Be destroyed
By being rude
Defiling joy

Although it seems
So hard to try
My nature says
I mustn't hide

So I am trapped
By only me
Not turning back
And never free

My Only Friend

My body begs me for sleep
My eyes beg for moisture
Which means
My mind and heart
Long for emotional pain
Or severe and thorough joy.

Does it make me crazy
To know that I need pain,
To know that I need tears,
To know that I need change?

I still want nothing
For I have it all
But sometimes I cry
For no reason,
And I cannot seem
To redeem those tears
When I need them most.

They, too, are unreliable
So my only friend remains
As I scribble phrase after
Meaningless phrase
Until I run out of ink.

Nervous Laughter

Picking
Shards of glass
From a
Broken picture frame

I am reminded
Of myself

I threw the splinters
The clear, clean,
Pure,
Razor-sharp splinters
Into a trash bag
Without any second thought.

A few seconds ago,
As I recalled
Being reminded of myself,
I laughed nervously.

Is it funny?
Not really.

Get Away

I am always cold,
My fingertips frozen.
Always.

My eyes are hazy.
My ears can ignore you,
My mind can be blank.
Never feel again.

My heart can be cold.
I could mean everything,
And nothing means anything
To me anymore.

I could be buried
Beneath all I portray
And really be
Someone completely different.

How would you know?
How would I know?

I need to get away,
From here,
From people,
From life....

From reality.

Lost In Thought

And all the world
Melts away to nothing
And floats away
As quickly as
One note gives way
To the next.

My universe
Exists now only
In whatever I am
Currently touching.

All that matters
Is the book, the pen
And the thoughts
Flowing magically
From my hand,
Forming familiar words
That don't really
Mean anything
Unless I can somehow
Wrap up the emotion
With the pen….

I have become
So lost,
Once again.

Repeated Confusion

And the questions
Keep repeating
In the room
That is my mind

And there are
Never any answers
To be given
Or received

The answers stay
Wherever they are hiding
And maybe the questions
Are not complete
Or clear enough

So the search
The quest, the mission
Continues on
Maybe for minutes
Maybe for
Decades longer

And perhaps
When it is found
Humanity
Will cease to exist,

For what are we
Without a purpose?

Without Reason

It all makes sense
Inside my head
But all the words
Cannot be fed

Onto the page
Fills me with rage
I can't contain
I must engage

In conversation
With myself
No relaxation
But far from hell

And if I had a reason
If only I had a reason

Any grounds at all
To feel what I have felt
Maybe I could
Break my fall

And maybe
I'll be well

But without reason
Doomed to fail
Sentenced to feel
Weak and small

Smiling at a Distance

Is something wrong?
Of course it's not
Never for me
But I never forgot

And it's always the same
But everything's changed
And I will remain
Trapped in my cage

Although I feel dumb
And stupid sometimes
It's never the same
But I'll always cry
About only myself

Because nobody else
Affects me that much
They're beginning to touch
But it's never enough

Sometimes I feel close
But so far away
I don't want to leave
But I don't want to stay

I am not aloof
I'm just paused for a while
And still
I manage to smile

Simplicity

And the feelings
Rush ashore
Making it sweeter
Making it pure

Things need to be simple
So they don't get confused
Confusion
Messes things up

Doomed to fail
If it gets too complicated
But emotions
Sometimes do that

And that is the time
When the simple truth
Matters the most
To keep things
From getting too confused

So be honest, be real
And admit what you feel
Even if you're unsure

Keep it simple,
Keep it pure

Optimism

Want to keep on going
Even when
Everything says stop.

Want to keep on driving
Even when
I don't know
What lies ahead.

Want to keep on trying
Even when
There's nothing
Left to try for.

Want to keep on living
Even when
It seems
The end is near.

Want to keep on smiling
Even when
It seems
So pointless.

Want to keep on going
Even when
The road runs out.

Trapped

Hide the meaning,
Kill the truth,
Suffer through
All that is you

And, looking back,
I am appalled
At what you are
And how quickly I fall

Into the trap
Of all you are

And still I love
But still I hate
And anger fills
And burns and grates....

What If

What if I run
And what if I hide?
What if I stay
Locked up deep inside?

What if I matter,
But what if I don't?
What if I try
When I usually won't?

What if the sun
Never shines anymore?
What if it rains
Until everything's warped?

What if my mind
Leaves me empty and cold?
What if it never
Returns to my soul?

What if my shell
Is just simply there?
What if I'm empty?
What if no one cares?

Warning

Fragile.
Do not drop.
Do not bend.
Do not break.
Do not betray.
Do not fuck over.

CAUTION!
Pressing of
Too many buttons
May cause
Permanent
Internal damage
To the merchandise.

Psychotic bitch
May appear
And beat your
Fucking face in
With a hammer!

Warning:
Back-stabbers in mirror
Are closer
(Much closer)
Than they appear.

In Reply to Nothing

Some say
It's always the quiet ones
That end up being psychotic....

I wonder
Just how true that is?

I shouldn't care
What people think,
But when people
Start to talk....
Ugh.

Whoever it's about
Will be chewed up
Swallowed
And regurgitated
A million times
Before everyone
Gets sick of that person,
Or something better
Comes along.

He said,
She said,
The wall said nothing
In reply to all their
Nothing.

Volume

Sometimes
It gets too loud.
Too much noise,
So I turn it down.

Sometimes
It's too quiet.
Then I get
A high-pitched
Ringing in my ears.

It's not because of where I am
Or who I am
Surrounded by.

I mean…
The thoughts scream,
And then they whisper,
And they expect me
To hear them all
And write them all down?

Fabulous.

So what happens next?
Will they leave me
Altogether,
And never, ever return?

Things Change

Words are untrue
And promises broken,
Nothing to do
But leave them unspoken.

Nothing is ever
The same for always,
There is no forever
And no one will stay.

Everyone goes away,
No matter what they say.

No matter how much
They pretend to care,
They never really do
And they always disappear.

Lack of Artistry

I lack the images
In my mind
And the skillful
Fingers

To draw a picture
Of any kind
Of any shape
Or texture

A face, a hand
Or even flowers
Nothing more
Than simple things

For I lack the talent
To draw the picture
I've painted
In my mind

With You

Make me fresh
And make me new
Start again
I'll start with you

Take the old
And toss it out
Cleanse my soul
Shut bad things out

Maybe I
Can make it good
Maybe we
Do what we should

Now it all
Falls back to place
How it is
With a new face

Make me fresh
And make me new
…
I'll start again with you

Jaded Washington

In the dark
The world is good
Peace and silence
What a place
What a time
On my face
On my mind

Hell above
Heaven below
What can love
Do for us now?

People talk
Never stop
To take in
The air again

Something perfect
Can't be found
Except in music
Feel the sounds

Making sense
Is overrated
Do I care
If this state is jaded?

Not the Only Way

Don't try to see
If you are blind

Don't try to feel
If you are numb
Don't force it
If you just don't know

Don't try to hear
If you are deaf
Don't try to speak
Without the words

Don't try to sing
Without a voice
Don't try to try
Without a choice

And don't give up
Unless you know
That it's the only way
… It's not

Mixed Up

Sometimes
Nothing seems to matter
Sometimes
Everything does

Sometimes
People make me crazy
But sometimes
That's all I've got

Sometimes
I want to curl up and die
Other times
I love everything

Sometimes
You really don't seem to know
But other times
You read my mind

Softer

I feel you running through me
Like sand through my fingers
I can feel your memories
Their bitterness still lingers

I taste the salt of your skin
And in it, the pain in your blood
I see the small warmth therein
You'd feel more if you could

You should know
That I'd live all of your pain
Just to see you
Free from your chains

I could inhale your aura
Die young with your smile
I would wander forever
And swim the length of the Nile

Just to see you
Escaping your prison
Just to know
You're safe from the rain

I feel you surging through me
With love, tears, and laughter
I can taste the melody
Of all your hatred... softer.

I Am, I'm Not

I am not special
But I am unique
I am not popular
But I am loved
I am not creative
But I am inspired
I am not talented
But I am an artist

I cannot sing
But I've found my voice
I cannot dance
But I have perfect rhythm
I cannot be judged
But I shoulder the blame
I cannot enjoy
But I can savor it.

I am not creative
But I am inspired

I am not special
But I am unique

Quickly Fading

Not a friend to betray
Not a soul to bring pain
Not an ear to confide in
But who cares anyway

Not a heart to feel
Not a mind to be real
Not a body to cut
Not empty nor full

Just a face
To disappear
Without a trace
Never near

Fading too quickly
Minutes tick by
Moments are sickly
And for them we cry

When all is finished
The battle subsides
The wounds never heal
Because everyone dies

Jagged Edges

Look in the mirror
And see what you see
A perfect reflection
Of you inside me

Shatter the mirror
To jagged-edged frames
Of hundreds of pictures
That are all the same

And all that we've done
Is just multiply
The love mixed with pain
Everything that's inside

Look in my eyes
You will see me inside
I have felt real pain
Although I am a child

As fragile as everything
Is or may seem
Does it really matter
If it's all a dream?

Can't Hate

The hesitation
In our conversation
Is killing my patience
And making me mad

Though inspiration
Is my creation
It becomes an invasion
Without invitation

The absence of hate
Closes the gates
But makes all of it grate
On my nerves all the time

Do I believe fate
Tried to step in too late
Or was it simply bait
To get me to wait?

When I think of you
I know it's the truth
And nothing you do
Can make me hate you

Up to You

It's lonely in this place
And cold
If only I could kiss your face
And have you here to hold

I cannot help but feel
Alone
If only I could start to heal
I want you to come home

And here I am again
Missing you with every breath
And there I lay again
Loving you with all I am

I want you to see me
To know
To understand how I can be
And see that I won't go

I cannot make you see
Or do
Anything for you or me
That's all up to you

Oblige & Conform

It seems so odd to me now
To do the things
I used to do
Because I haven't
In so long.

I didn't want to change,
But I changed for you.
The smallest things remain,
But the rest was all for you.

You molded me
Into your perfect little wife.
I hate you for that,
But I still love you for life,
Which makes me hate myself.

Your words cut deep,
Your anger spreads like fire;
I fear it.

Your fuse is short,
And so I simply
Oblige to you and
Conform to who you
Want me to be.

No more.

I love you,
But I love me, too.

Somewhere Between

The emptiness is fleeting
And the moments will decay
Everyone keeps leaving
I don't want to go away

My heart feels full yet empty
And my mind keeps me in check
If it wasn't for this heartache
I fear my brain would crack

I can't focus my emotions
I feel horrible inside
I don't want to be so distant
But I can't help but hide

Since we've been together
I've grown colder toward my friends
I sit and think and wonder
If that feeling will ever end

I still don't feel like me
And I don't like who I've become
I've lost myself somewhere between
Love, hurt, and being numb

Pulling in Opposite Directions

I'd rather be alone
Than constantly in pain.
I'd rather have no one
Than feel that way again.

I know you don't mean
To make me feel bad
But you do anyway
And I'm constantly sad

The things I write you
Are not all true
I'm so angry with you
But I don't want to

Don't want you to worry
Don't want you to cry
Don't want you to feel bad
'Cause I know you try.

2:00 AM Again

It's 2:00 AM again
And I am here alone
Just like I've always been
Even when you're home

It's 2:00 AM again
Can't help but think of you
And just how long it's been
All the pain you've put me through

And I'm still here
Why am I still here?
The truth is clear
I didn't see it before
This even you can't ignore

It's 2:00 AM again
And things are looking gray
Why can't you understand?
Should I go or should I stay?

It's 2:00 AM again
Emotions running high
Who will take the blame
For all the tears I've cried?

And I'm still here
Why am I still here?
The truth is clear
I didn't see it before
This even you can't ignore

It's 2:00 AM again
Sleep seems far away
But all I've ever been
I am, so it's okay

It's 2:30 now
And I know it's on its way
For now, all I can do
Is curiously wait….

Bleeding

It rolled down my cheek
And it smelled like blood
A drop on my lips
And it tasted like blood

A part of my soul
Is dying again
Bleeding out the windows
And cleansing my skin

I'm bleeding for you
And I've already died
Now it's all true
And you never even tried

Mine & Yours

Mine is my world
Is my love, is my happiness
Yours is my pain
And my hurt

Mine is my sun
And my stars, and my confidence
Yours are my scars
And my tears

Mine is my life
Is my name, is my joy in it
Yours is the rain
From my sky

Mine is my mind
My desire, my contentment
Yours are the knives
In my heart

Mine is my poetry
My words, which you robbed me of
Yours are the many
Blank books

Mine is the art
Is the canvas of wretched thoughts
Your thoughtless words
Have provoked

Mine is the gift
Of my love, which I gave to you
Yours are the shards
That remain

Questions

Will I go or will I stay?
Will my mind rot and decay?
Will my heart go numb and cold?
Will I feel bruised and old?

Or will I be content?
Happiness until the end?
Will I feel like I am found?
Will my pain fall to the ground?

Will you prove to me you are
Everything I'll ever need?
Will our love find who we are
So we can simply be?

Will you let me down again?
Will I live like I did then?
Will the tears flow from my heart
Until I find the strength to part?

Will I stop longing for
All the happiness I had before?
Or will I still regret
Everything I can't forget?

Yin & Yang

We are a myriad of thoughts
In a kaleidoscope of dreams
And everything seems real
But nothing's what it seems

The evil that we do
Is for the good of all we know
And when there's no evil left
Then there's nowhere left to go

The Complicated Choice Between Freedom & the Noose

My veins are made of nicotine
And caffeine flowing through
Gives motion to the wondering
About the things I do

The late nights and the sunrise
Companions through my life
At home inside the disguise
And hidden from the light

Ambivalent and tortured
Between this life and the last
Never knowing for sure
About my future past

The animal must choose
Between the wild and free outdoors
The freedom or the noose
Made of love and happiness

Another Step in the Opposite Direction

The paint on my walls
Chips and peels away
Slowly crumbling
Weathered with age
And emotion

The tiny cracks spread
Across my skin
Like dried rivers
And I watch myself
Falling apart

So painfully and slowly
Bit by bit
I crumble at your feet
Right before your eyes
And you simply
Take another step
In the opposite direction

Out of sight
Out of mind…

Yet I see myself
More clearly now
And the cracks
Spider web into
Something beautiful

Lonely Face

And there she was
The quiet night
Sitting still
Not there, not quite

And there it lay
The broken vase
The water spilled
It met her gaze

And eyes stared
Into other eyes
As flowers framed
Their pretty face

The knees buckle
The fingers shake
And all the while
She's wide awake

Without a sound
It screams at her
And still, somehow
The voice is heard

Yet through the screams
The laughter rings
Mocking dreams
The silence sings

Many nights
Were spent this way
When all the light
Seems to dissipate

But soon the eyes
Evaporate
And all that's left
Is her lonely face

A Simple Pleasure

Thoughts are shared
And feelings spoken
Some are whole
And some are broken

Some are full
And some are rare
Some are abstract
Some just there

But I value these things
Because they seem real
They make my life better
And for them I feel

And as time ticks by
It's moving too fast
I want this forever
I want it to last

The Present Held Captive

With the past behind me
And the future still to come,
The present is all I have
To work with.
It sits at my feet
Like a lump of clay,
But I can't seem to form it
Into what I want it to be.

It's there; I can see it.
But it's shapeless,
Nothing in particular.
It has decades of potential
And eons of history,
A capacity for knowledge
Like a sponge for liquid,
And maybe the problem
Lies not in the clay
But in me, in my hands,
Maybe in my melancholy.

Maybe my procrastination
Will be the death of me,
My hands never reaching
To mold my clay.

Maybe I'm afraid
Of making it wrong,
Of making it as hideous
As I have become,
Or maybe I have to
Search for my hands,
If they've been chopped off
Or tied behind my back.

Maybe my captor is me.

Purple

My world is purple upside down
But I don't know what color it is
Right side up...
It's been so long, and I forgot

Situation's getting worse
So in my mind, I need a hearse
To carry these broken bones
In this bag of battered flesh
Because the shape
Has been misplaced,
Lost somewhere

I need to stand on solid ground
But I haven't found my footing yet
So, spinning madly, I will fall
Until I hit rock bottom

I'll lay there
Maybe I will heal
But then I can find my footing
And be planted
Solidly on the ground

Until I trip and fall again

Ambivalence

The silence outside
And the noise in my head
Are an interesting combination

I can't seem to find
My will to feel glad
That's not a good realization

So this may go on
For quite some time
And no one can bring consolation

And I will just yawn
But I have to find
Myself in this odd constellation

A Clever Way Out

Razorblade or knife
Peeling skin
Away from flesh,
Like removing
A sticker…

Latex fingers
Latex body
Falls apart
In the mirror

Gazing into
Blue eyes
No face left
And secular ugliness
Is soon to follow

Want to be destroyed
From the inside out
But the walls
Are in my way

No one can get in
And I cannot get out
No escape from here

It's internal
I'm internalized
Have to devise
A clever way out of myself

Reflection

It said to her,
"Look up.
I'm beautiful,
And I'm a reflection
Of you."

It smiled down and
It lit the way,
And as she began to cry,
It began to rain.

The tears streamed down,
The thunder crashed,
And suddenly, she felt the urge
To fly away forever,
Maybe go somewhere
More beautiful than she

And take it in
In gasps of awe,
Without ever knowing
That it wasn't real.

She can feel her bones here,
The weight of all her sorrow,
Jabbing her body
And beating it into submission.

So when it smiles,
It smiles inside
So no one else can see,
And so does she.

Black Roses

We are like
The fields of black roses
My mind drifts into
When I feel alone.

We are dark
And beautiful,
Different and free;
We cannot be tamed
Nor caged, nor bred,
Nor can we be
Reproduced.

We are unapproachable,
Loved and hated
All at once.

Sometimes our thorns
Outnumber our blooms,
And we cannot be changed.

We'd rather be alone
Than risk being trampled upon.

We'd rather be strong and lonely
Than vulnerable
To anyone.

We are like black roses.

Contradictory Purpose

I am like
The incomplete
That fulfills
The incomplete

I am like
The broken
That helps to fix
The broken

I am like
The weakness
That strengthens
All their weakness

I am like
A rock
Made of
Nothing like a rock

I am like a secret
That everybody knows

I cannot roam the physical world
So I roam another
I wander through people
There for a short while
Longer for others

Passing over everyone
Never fully comfortable
Always wanting more

Taste

I liked the way my fingers looked,
Pressed against your lips.

I liked the way your hands felt,
Enveloping my face.

I liked the way you calmly
Kissed my fingertips.

… And I like
The way you taste.

The Lion & the Crab

There is a lion residing in a crab's small shell
Avoiding serious confrontation
If in the least way possible
Sometimes the lion
Comes down with a case of
Cabin fever
And needs to get out
And run, play, hunt
Hunt for food
Hunt for confrontation

It sort of fell in my lap
This particular one
It was bound to happen
Sooner or later,
Just chose to happen sooner.

This lion has been
Restless as of late,
And comes out more often now.
So it emerged
At the right moment,
When the crab was thinking
Angry thoughts,
And the lion helped
To alleviate this madness,
Although the crab
Had advised against it.

Too late
The confrontation has
Already taken place,
And the lion won't admit it,
But she did go a bit far.

The crab will pay
The consequences;
That's always
How it goes.

When the lion's had her fill,
She goes back to sleep,
And the crab is left
To clean up all the mess
The lion's made.

The crab is not
Courageous, nor angry,
Nor outspoken.
The crab is very docile,
Even when her heart is broken.

The lion slumbers
Deep inside
While all this is taking place,
But the lion's also
Full of pride,
More powerful than her disgrace.

Invasion of the Face

The pictures on the wall
All seem to say the same thing,
And they have the same
Effect on me
Every time I see them.
It creeps up slowly,
Taking me by surprise,
Then takes over
My face and
My heart.

Most of these pictures
Are of the same
Piece of my life
As most of the pictures
In the albums.

I feel the sting
In my eyes first;
Then the tightness
In my throat,
As the muscles
In my face
Stretch themselves out,
Feeling almost alien,
A strange invasion
That makes me lose
Control;

And my lips slowly form
Into a smile.

Salty Eternity

The tide washes over her
And as she is
Enveloped and
Swept away
By this salty eternity,
She can taste
The bittersweet of it all,
Melting away before her eyes.

After the initial shock
Of icy fingers
Touching every inch of her,
She suddenly feels
A warm glow,
Like a dagger of light
In a darkened room,
It pierces her heart
And she is no longer cold.

Filled from the inside out
With a warm, syrupy feeling,
Her body and mind
Relax,
And she is beautiful,
Swept from the world,
Swept from reality,
And carried away
On this decadence,
This cloud of melting light.

Peace.

Choking

It built upon itself
Stacking layers slowly
So no one would notice
Or care

Could it be any more
Obvious
To the mind in which
This occurs?

Stacks and piles and layers
Muffling all goodness
Burying patience
Making it hard to listen

The silence is
What brings on madness
The pressure is
What nurtures insanity

Eventually, a tolerance is built up
And it will pile up
Too high to get out

Inevitably,
Death will soon follow
For lack of oxygen

Do You See?

Are you blind
Or do you see?
Do you see
The world like me?
Or is everything
Depressing,
Your darkness
Obscuring any hope
You may have had left
In your bitter soul?

Are you deaf
Or can you hear?
Do you hear
That painful scream,
Or the secret
Happiness within?
Do you hear
The noisy café,
Or the joy
Of being surrounded
By friends?

Are you blind
Or do you see?
Do you see
The world like me?

Exhausted Spirit

So tired,
But unable to sleep.
Maybe it's
The spirit
That's exhausted,
Not the physical self.

Eyes stinging
From tears shed in the past;
Head pounding
From too many thoughts
Intruding,
Forcing their way in,
Like a mind-rape
Has occurred.

Heart aching,
Now numb
From too much pain
Surfacing at once.

Yet still there are
No answers,
No solutions
Have been found.

Slipping Away

Like the calm before a storm,
My sullen demeanor is eerie
I won't be able to
Hold it back much longer,
For how can I keep
Pretending that
This guilt and your pain
Don't bother me?

How can I keep
Ignoring my own needs
When I'm slipping away
To insanity?

Ever so slowly,
One layer at a time,
My self is being
Drawn away,
Pieces already gone

To a state of mind
That is more dangerous
Than your anger
Holding a gun.

So, which one
Scares me more?

False Hope

Apologizing for who we are,
We make up in hopes
That the magic of love
Will be the glue to
Keep us together forever.

I cannot heal your wounds,
And you cannot set me free,
So we'll dance eternally
In this belief that we,
The trapped and melancholy,
Can somehow muster
The strength to bury

Our true selves….

Finally Home

And here,
Among the
Burgundy waters
And the
Attention-stealing,
Beautiful children,
Home surrounds
Everyone.

Not simply a house,
But a place to feel
Safe,
To belong.

Everyone
Deserves to feel
This happy,
Finally home,
Finally back
Where we belong.

Beautiful bliss;
Peaceful,
Safe.

Healing

The bleeding has
Ceased now,
The endless red
From scabs that
Never fully healed…

They are now
One step closer
To becoming
Mere scars,
Distant memories
Of a life once lived.

Rejoicing now,
In my mind I
Celebrate,
This beautiful release
Of all the guilt
You made me feel.

Never-Ending Journey

Trying to find yourself
Is like trying to find proof
That there is a God…

Ever-changing,
Evolving,
Mutating…
We are never
The same person twice.

This is the quest,
The endless search,
The never-ending journey.

This is life,
And nothing
Is more beautiful.

Freedom

Stuck in that place
That oppressing life;
And all I ever wanted
Was to be happy…

I loved you;
In some ways, I still do…
But now,
You've lost your precious
Control over me,
Over the situation.

I still ask myself
Why I went back to you,
And the answer is so simple:

I thought you would change.
I loved you,
And I thought things might be
Better for us…

For a while,
The weather was
Beautiful;
Warm and bright,
Untainted by
Any clouds in the sky.

Then everything
Went back to how it was.
My discontent,
And all your
Negative everything.

I know that I am destined
For something so much more;
And all you ever wanted
Was to keep me in a cage.

So I broke free.

Happy Again

Half sunshine
And half rain,
Mostly pleasure
But some pain

Can't believe
How good it feels
To just be whole
And simply live

Gluing pieces
Back together
I don't know why
We said forever

You married me
Admittedly
For the tiny
Life inside

But I didn't need you
I came close once
I thought I needed you,
But now I see again

I never needed you
The blindfold has now
Been removed
And I am fine again

And slowly,
The chains are falling
The weight is lifting

A million pounds
Of pressure gone

And I can breathe again
I can be me again
I am happy again
I feel free again

Paranoia

And then there was a calm
A serenity so unlikely
A tranquility to be suspicious of
And there was still paranoia

Checking the rearview
And watching the cars
Are they following,
Spying, private investigators?

Are you a true threat,
Or are you just crazy
And I'm over-estimating
Your anger, rage, intelligence?

Or am I being
Overly dramatic and
Paranoid and scared,
A drama queen, as you say?

Or are you capable
Of all the things,
All the threats and violence
That I give you credit for?

Pain in the Joy

It seemed so real,
It seemed so true;
It seemed to final,
To be with you…

Some times were good,
Some times were bad.
Some moments horrid,
Pushed out of my head…

Now I'm being asked
To deal with it all at once;
And part of me is happy,
But part of me still hurts.

And come to find
It was all a lie;
The life you gave me
Was never mine…

And I now know
What fueled your rage,
Why you were angry,
Why I was caged…

I felt so small,
So weak and unloved;
Felt so trapped
And guilty and bruised…
But I know why
You treated me bad,
And I hope you know
All we could've had…

I finally found
The strength to leave;
My will to survive,
My need to breathe…

And I can see
How awful you were,
But I can't understand
Why leaving still hurts…

And I can be
Who I really am,
But how did I ever
Fall into your hands?

I know how you were,
But leaving still hurt.

The Song (Before There Was You)

Before there was you
I could talk to anyone
Before there was you
I had never known fear

Before there was you
I had no complications
Before there was you
I let people be near

And now, I find myself afraid
To let anyone in
And now, I find myself betrayed
By what I believed in
And how can I be
So affected by you
When I finally see
That your words were untrue...

Before there was you
I was happy alone
Before there was you
My life was still my own

Before there was you
I was never afraid
Before there was you
I didn't feel so enraged

And now that we're over
Now that it's done
I'm facing a storm
Of memories gone

It seems like a bad dream
A nightmare at best
How do I heal myself?
How do I find rest?

When there was you
I was never myself
When there was you
I gave up all control

And now that it's done
I feel lost and alone
Now that it's done
I am finally home
Our life was a lie
And I thought it was true
But that's what I get
For truly loving you

Emotional Power

And so it came to be
That independence
And self-assurance,
Confidence and
Beauty,
Have all been restored
To their rightful place.

The mind still wanders back,
But memories seem
Strangely distant,
Emotions still attached,
Yet somehow disconnected.

Insanity still
Seems to stalk the prey,
And what a fragile thing
The mind can be...
How easily destroyed.

The victim is everyone,
But no one is victimized;
At least not purposely.
Accidental victimhood.

Could it be
That eyes don't really see,
Ears don't really hear,
Skin can't really feel...
The only sense
That truly gives the mind
Something to work with
Is an emotional sense...?

For everything
Comes down to one:
The heart.

Issues Surfacing

So unexpected,
So ill-prepared…

The trust issues
Now surfacing
In the face of
Your sincerity.

Uncertainty
And doubt
Come into subtle being,
As words are exchanged
And understanding
Is attempted…

How did something
So beautiful
Become such a disgrace?

And all that's left
Is her lonely face.

Breaking the Silence

The .45 was loaded
And I never said a word
It's time to break the silence
My screams will now be heard

The .45 was loaded
And I locked it in my mind
Mum about your violence
Not a word unkind

Your .45 was loaded
As your nervous laugh escaped
You tried to say it was a joke
As two of us were raped

Your .45 was loaded
When you abandoned them
The children whom you said you loved
Won't ever see you again

My .45 is loaded
As I reconstruct my life
I never needed anyone
Didn't have to be your wife

My .45 is loaded
As I battle every fear
One by one they're falling
I'll shed no more tears

The .45 was loaded
But your power now is lost
How does it feel to lose control?

Was it worth the cost?

I hope so.
Just remember:
God is counting my tears.
They'll be waiting for you,
If you ever make it there.

Superficial Apathy

What a mess
I have become…
What a life,
What a
Complicated situation,
Always getting worse,
And I,
So seemingly okay,
Hide it all so well
In superficial apathy.

Heart in a Jar

And there it was.
Undefined, yet stubborn,
There it was.

Exposed and vulnerable,
Open to hope and,
Therefore, open to hurt.
There it was.

But, kept in a jar,
The openness was
To no avail...

For, no matter
How open-minded,
It's the open heart
That needs to feel.

The mind can be
As open as they come,
But the heart is in a jar.

The Worst Kind of Pain

Would it still
Melt me to my core
If you looked at me
The way you did
With those eyes?

The eyes that told
Of so much pain
Without speaking
Without hesitation

You never faltered
In your gaze
Nor did you falter
In your anger—
So quick to turn

And now, here I am
Thinking back to
My time with you
My love for you

And a cold chill
Runs through me
As I realize again
That I can never
Be with you forever

Tell me why it hurts
This never-ending ache
At how much I care
Even after everything

Confusion is
The worst kind of pain.

Within

And in some moment
Within what is called time
I can feel my senses
Beginning to crumble

And in some instance
Within what is called life
My mind will try
To burn my flesh

And in some second
Within what is called minute
My emotions will overtake
Any logical reasoning

But in this moment
Within what is called existence
All of that storm
Has already passed…

In one second.

No Happy Medium

Complicated life
For a complicated girl.
Emotions
Weave intricate patterns
Made of various
Highs and lows.

Situations
Are either good
And wonderful
To the extreme,
Or as dire as
They dare to be.

Why is it always
So extreme?
There's no
Happy medium.

Set Me Free

Being me
In a world full of you
Is the hardest thing
I've ever had to do.

Leaving you
So that I could be me
Was hard as well
But will set me free.

Simply Me

Once upon a time,
She was me and I was she,
But did that mean I wasn't me?
I had so many uncertainties.
Anxiety had let me be,
But sadness never felt a need…
To leave.

Some time went by for she and I,
And I and she,
And now, my friends, I guarantee
That she's not me
And I'm not she…

Now, I'm simply me.

Funny (Not Funny Ha-Ha)

Funny how a phrase
Can capture a heart,
Even when that heart
Will never stay captured.

Funny how life
Can suck you in
And, at the same time,
Drain your very soul.

Funny how all can be well
And, the very next day,
Disaster and chaos
Could rip you apart without mercy.

Funny how indecisive
And nervous people get
When we're all alike,
The same on the inside.

Funny how we always want
The opposite of what we have,
When we wanted
What we have at some point.

Funny…
But not funny ha-ha.

True Joy

The sky was bruised today
And I had nothing left to say
I've been learning how to fly
So I can leave myself behind

When everything's been broken
It seems difficult to breathe
And every word you've spoken
Feels unheard and unbelieved

Every soul has picked up pieces
After watching them get shattered
Empty words and hollow kisses
The illusion that you mattered

And as I watched the bruised sky
Turn into twinkling night
My tears dissolved into the air
In hopes that there's true joy out there

Darkness Catching Up

The sky was bipolar
Again today,
Charcoal clouds
Rolling in
From the
West,
Bringing on
An instant darkness.

By 7:45,
It was night,
Black darkness,
Pouring rain
In buckets
From the sky.

It's as though
The rain that had been
Lacking in the summer
All poured down
Today.

Would You?

Would you believe me
If I told you
That I need you?

Would you love me
If I told you
That I'm yours?

Would you stay
If I told you
I won't make it?

Would you hear me
If I screamed
Inside my head?

Would you hold me
If I told you
That I'm broken?

Would you save me
If I fell
Apart again?

Would you help me
If I lost
My heart somewhere?

Would you cry with me?
Would you laugh with me?
Would you die with me?
Would you fly with me?

Realization

As I drove home
On the 90
From Coeur d'Alene,
All I could think of
Was you.

As I packed the suitcase
And loaded the car
Earlier this morning,
All I could think of
Was you.

As I sat at the diner,
Trying to squeeze out
Any drop of inspiration,
All I could think of
Was you.

As I lie awake,
The rest of the house
Is fast asleep,
All I can think of
Is you.

And as I do this,
Unable to sleep,
Kept awake by my mind,
I realize
You've not returned
Any of my calls today.

Loud Silence

Hair stands on end
At the chilly touch
Of air outside…

The silence
Is so loud
That a whisper could be
Heard for miles,
But a scream
Would drown in it.

Seven

It took hold briefly;
Only seven tears were shed,
Only seven tears escaped,
And then I felt okay.

Not sure how to feel;
Only finding reasons not to,
Only seven moments pass
And nothing seems to stay.

Only in times of weakness
Do I seem to care or
Be affected by the
Everyday affliction…

… Of loneliness.

Only seven minutes,
Seven thoughts of misery.
Seven pieces of my soul,
Only seven tears escaped.

Only seven moments,
Seven broken feelings…
Seven new cracks in my heart,
Seven screaming reasons…

… Not to want to feel.

Storm

Frightening and beautiful,
This fierce expression of
Nature's unforgiving rage.
Violent and sporadic,
Unpredictable; chaotic.

Angry winds force
Entire tree lines to obey
Their every destructive whim.

Strong gusts tossing
Anything they can
Into the side of the house,
And onto the roof…

Meanwhile, I just sit and hope
That we will all be okay,
And wish for it to end.

Boom

Self-discovery.
Exploration of the
Constant battle within,
The battle of
Yourself vs. Yourself.

This alone is enough
To drive anyone into
A deep and dangerous
Madness...
Even insanity.

Are you ready?

Prepare yourself for
The collision that is
Bound to come...

The unavoidable crash of
Mind, soul, and heart.

BOOM.

Lessons in Oxymoron Form

It's hard to wrap
Your mind around
How easy it is
To lose yourself.

It's difficult to see
How different you become,
How compromised you are
When you're blinded by someone.

It's strange to be aware
Of your intellect and wisdom
But still be drawn into
A trap of drama and confusion.

It's such a contradiction;
Easy to trust someone else,
But I couldn't seem to follow
My own heart, my intuition.

So that was the lesson
Which I was meant to learn;
To trust myself above all others
Or I just might get burned.

Chunks of My Heart

I chopped off my hair
In a screaming attempt
To rebel against your control.
You broke my heart
Every day
And I escaped, got away
As far and as fast
As my car would take me.
Broken and bruised,
My heart lay
In shattered icy chunks
All over our kitchen floor,
With bits and pieces
Scattered in the bathroom
Where your .45
Pressed against my face;
Cold, hard, angry metal
On flushed, damp skin...
My skin.

Anxiety
Even now, my heart
Feels bloated and
Off-beat at
This cruel memory
...
Will I ever
Stop shaking?

Strong Smile

Always stay strong.
Never give up,
Never give in.
Do not let
Your smile falter…
Do not let it fade.

For this smile
Holds many things.
It represents strength,
It represents confidence.
It means pride,
Determination,
Contentment,
Happiness,
And motivation.

When I wear my smile,
It's because my soul
Is smiling.
My heart is
Flying high,
And my dreams
Are in my reach.

The Epilogue Poem

My words
Have been heard,
For once
Not ignored...
Relieved,
Not deceived,
Invited
To believe
That my soul
Is still whole....

As fractured
As it seemed.
Has my love
Been redeemed,
Or is this
Just a dream?

Confusion
And fear,
All dwell here...
Whispered softly
In our ears
And adding fuel
To our tears,
Only to
Discover
No one
Will recover
Once their soul
Has a hole,
And their heart
Falls apart

At such an
Agonizing
....
Lack of speed.

What, then, exactly
Do we need
To succeed
In endeavors
Of the heart,
Mind,
And soul?
Is the hole
Really there,
Does it matter
If you care?

If your answer
Is yes,
Please confess...
And profess
Your true self,
Whether ill
Or in good health,
Every heart
Has its moment....

Loneliness
Can make a mess
Of tidiness.

No matter how OCD
We may be,
Everyone,
Including me,
Has their needs
That need meeting,

Never ceasing
The quest
To finally
Find what is best,
Deeming all the rest
Meaningless.

Will anyone
Under the sun
Ever stop
Searching
Once they have
Begun?
Will these poor
Nomadic souls
Find their place,
Though never whole?

Forever wandering around,
If you are lost, can you be found?
Will you eventually stand on the ground?
Or does everyone
Keep falling down?

When you feel
Like you belong,
Please let me know,
So I can come.

About the Author

Jennifer-Crystal Johnson is originally from Germany, but was raised in numerous places. She has published one novella under her former last name, *The Outside Girl: Perception is Reality* (Publish America, 2005 - out of print), a poetry book, *Napkin Poetry* (Broken Publications, 2010, second edition 2016), and a collection of poetry, art, and prose called *Strangers with Familiar Faces* (Broken Publications, 2011). More recently, Jen published *If You're Human Don't Open the Door* (Broken Publications, 2012), *Our Capacity for Evil* (Broken Publications, 2015), both collections of short horror stories, and her first science fiction novel, *Fibers*, book one of the Infiltration Trilogy.

Her poem, Yin & Yang, was featured on Every Writer's Resource's Poem a Day site, along with two other poems. One of her short stories, The Huntress, was featured in Zombie Coffee Press (no longer online), and another short horror story, Simple Truth, was published on Every Writer's Resource. Her poetry has appeared in various anthologies. She currently works as a freelance writer and editor as well as helping other authors self-publish their own books.

She lives in the Pacific Northwest with her three kids, three cats, and their puppy, Thor. Her domestic violence anthology can be found at www.SoulVomit.com and her publishing company is Broken Publications. She recently began creating video tutorials about how to self-publish, which can be found at No Bull Self-Publishing. Last but not least, she recently started an anthology called *Beneath the Veil of Night*. Submission guidelines and links for the first three themes can be found on the Submissions page at www.BrokenPublications.com.

www.ingramcontent.com/pod-product-compliance
Lightning Source LLC
Chambersburg PA
CBHW060156070426
42447CB00033B/1706